Love & Logic®
Teacher-isms

Love & Logic®
Teacher-isms

by Jim Fay and Charles Fay, Ph.D.

Love and Logic®
INSTITUTE, Inc.

www.loveandlogic.com • 1-800-338-4065

The Love and Logic Institute, Inc.
2207 Jackson Street, Golden, CO 80401-2300
www.loveandlogic.com

First edition
First printing, 2001
Published and printed in the United States of America

ISBN 1-930429-17-7

Library of Congress Number: 2001095026

BOOK PRODUCTION AND DESIGN:

Carol Thomas, project coordinator

Michael Snell, Shade of the Cottonwood, Topeka, KS
cover design and interior design

Paula Niedrach Botkin, illustrations

LOVE AND LOGIC®

Easy to Learn

Life Changing

Raises Responsible Kids

INTRODUCTION

There is no journey more exciting, packed with potential peril, and more fulfilling than teaching. With great caring, dedication, and skill, teachers change lives every single day!

If you've ever attended a Love and Logic® seminar with Jim Fay, Foster W. Cline, M.D., or Charles Fay, Ph.D., you know that their speeches are full of captivating and inspiring insights about teaching. You also know how fast these spontaneous truths flow from their lips...and how difficult it is to capture all of them in your notes.

For years, educators have asked us for a book filled with these simple, yet powerful thoughts...thoughts that remind teachers how important they really are...and thoughts that provide common-sense solutions to the day-to-day challenges of teaching.

It is with great pride that we have selected 101 of these "Wise Words." As you read each page, know that your dedication to reaching and teaching children makes the world a better place each and every day. Thanks for making a difference!

— THE EDITORS OF LOVE AND LOGIC

Jim Fay is one of America's most sought-after presenters in the area of parenting and school discipline. His background includes 31 years as a teacher and administrator, 20 as a professional consultant and public speaker, and many years as the parent of three children.

Jim is internationally recognized as a speaker and consultant to schools, parent organizations, counselors, mental health organizations, and the U.S. military. He is the author of more than 100 articles, books, audios, CD's, and videotapes on parenting and discipline. His infectious spirit and sense of humor have made him a popular personality on radio and television talk shows.

Charles Fay, Ph.D. is a

parent, author, business owner and consultant
to schools, parent groups and mental health
professionals around the world. His expertise
in developing and teaching practical discipline
strategies has been refined through work with
severely disturbed youth in school, hospital and
community settings. Charles has developed an
acute understanding of the most challenging

students. Having grown up with Love and Logic, he also provides a
unique...and often humorous...perspective.

WHAT IS LOVE AND LOGIC®

Love allows children to grow through their mistakes.

Logic allows children to live with the consequences of their choices.

THE LOVE AND LOGIC PROCESS

1. *Shared control: Gain control by giving away the control you don't need.*

2. *Shared thinking and decision-making: Provide opportunities for the child to do the greatest amount of thinking and decision-making.*

3. *Equal shares of consequences with empathy: An absence of anger causes a child to think and learn from his/her mistakes.*

4. *Maintain the child's self-concept: Increased self-concept leads to improved behavior and improved achievement.*

Teachers who smile and greet kids
at their door...each and every morning...
have students who give them more
to smile about...each and every evening.

Love and Logic Institute, Inc. • 1-800-338-4065

*Great teachers
save lives every day!*

*Wise teachers know that
the way they act is far more important
than what they say.*

*Never expect students
to be more excited about learning
than their teachers.*

How do we solve the truancy problem?
Make sure that schools meet
basic needs for respect, control, and
competence...better than street gangs.

Wise teachers know that
they can do everything right with
a student and still not see
that student succeed in their class.

Love and Logic Institute, Inc. • 1-800-338-4065

Don't criticize yourself, get down,
or lose hope. Instead, pat yourself
on the back for doing everything
within your power to help.

Who should be thinking the hardest about discipline in your school, the teachers or their students?

Wise teachers often ask, "How are you going to solve this problem?" They know that kids who solve their own problems become adults who create fewer problems for the world.

When a student leaves you speechless,
experiment with saying, "I'm going to have to do
something about this. We'll talk tomorrow."

Love and Logic Institute, Inc. • 1-800-338-4065

Saying, "We'll talk later…after I've given this more thought" is typically more effective than yelling, "That's it! You've just earned after-school detention…for life! I mean it!"

Love and Logic Institute, Inc. • www.loveandlogic.com

Teachers who use anger count the days until June. Those who use empathy count the lives they have changed.

Love and Logic Institute, Inc. • 1-800-338-4065

When a student complains,
"Why'd you give me that grade?"
Love and Logic teachers ask,
"Do I give you grades? Or am I just
the scorekeeper?"

Love and Logic Institute, Inc. • 1-800-338-4065

*Reasoning with an angry student is
like fighting fire with gasoline.*

Love and Logic Institute, Inc. • www.loveandlogic.com

Angry kids need space and time...
the only things that can douse the flames.

Love and Logic Institute, Inc. • 1-800-338-4065

Pencils are never lost...they're always "stolen." And it's always somebody else who "started it."

Great teachers know the difference between what they can and cannot control. We can't make kids have good "attitudes," but we stand a good chance of instilling them with ours.

Love and Logic Institute, Inc. • 1-800-338-4065

"I listen to people who raise their hands"
produces a better result than,
"Raise your hands."

Students will always need the same number of reminders or warnings they are given. Smart teachers set the limit once and follow through with actions instead of lectures.

During the first days of school, wise teachers show their students how to walk quietly in the hall, follow directions, sharpen pencils without making a scene, use the bathroom pass without interrupting the class, etc.

During the early days of school, unwise teachers never teach the behaviors they expect.

Love and Logic Institute, Inc. • www.loveandlogic.com

*Wise educators never expect a cafeteria
full of students to be quieter than a
cafeteria full of teachers.*

Love and Logic Institute, Inc. • 1 - 8 0 0 - 3 3 8 - 4 0 6 5

Effective teachers spend most of their energy preventing problems.

Ineffective teachers spend most of their energy reacting to problems.

Love and Logic Institute, Inc. • 1-800-338-4065

*Children with lice and runny noses
always want the most hugs.*

*A quality teacher-student relationship
means more than the combined power
of all teaching and discipline
techniques known to humankind.*

*Always turn sideways when talking
with an angry student. You become less
threatening, you're a smaller target,
and you can run away faster!*

Love and Logic Institute, Inc. • www.loveandlogic.com

Hearing, "You're sooo weird" from a teenager is actually a great comment.

Love and Logic Institute, Inc. • 1 - 8 0 0 - 3 3 8 - 4 0 6 5

Find something good about a difficult student, describe it in a letter, and send it to the parent. See how much grief this saves you later.

Love and Logic Institute, Inc. • www.loveandlogic.com

*Nobody cares how much we
know…until they know
how much we care.*

Love and Logic Institute, Inc. • 1-800-338-4065

A fun little sign to have in your classroom: "I schedule arguments at 12:15 p.m. and 3:15 p.m. daily"

Love and Logic Institute, Inc. • www.loveandlogic.com

When a child whines, "But you only argue at lunch and after school!" experiment with grinning and whispering, "I know."

*Wise teachers know that it takes two
to have a power struggle.*

Love and Logic Institute, Inc. • www.loveandlogic.com

Experiment with smiling at
a misbehaving student and asking,
"Could you save that behavior for
Mr. Tanner's room? Thank you."

When a child says "Not fair," smart teachers whisper, "I respect you too much to argue."

Wise teachers respond to a whiney
"But why?" with "If you don't figure
that out by next week I'll explain it."

Love and Logic Institute, Inc. • 1-800-338-4065

The Love and Logic classroom motto: The person who makes the problem gets to solve the problem.

The most important problem-solving rule:
Feel free to solve your problem in any way that
doesn't make a problem for someone else.

Love and Logic Institute, Inc. • 1-800-338-4065

Kids work hardest for the teachers
they love and respect.

Questions create thinking…warnings,
lectures, and threats create resistance.

Love and Logic Institute, Inc. • www.loveandlogic.com

"Is this the right place for that behavior?" creates thinking -
"Stop that or you're going to have to leave" creates resistance.

Love and Logic Institute, Inc. • 1-800-338-4065

*Love and Logic teachers have been
known to say, "The good news is that
I like students the same, regardless of
the grades they decide to earn."*

Students arrive on time for teachers
who meet them at the door, smile, and say,
"I'm glad you're here!"

Love and Logic Institute, Inc. • www.loveandlogic.com

*A Great Teacher: Firm limits
and high expectations…delivered
in a caring way.*

Love and Logic Institute, Inc. • 1-800-338-4065

Wise teachers know that the more small choices they provide, the fewer big problems they have.

Love and Logic teachers give 99% of
their choices when times are sweet...
so they can get away with saying,
"This time you don't get a choice"
when times turn sour.

Wise teachers give choices only on matters that won't cause a problem for themselves or others.

The art of giving effective choices:
Always offer two options, either of which
will make you deliriously happy.

Love and Logic Institute, Inc. • 1 - 8 0 0 - 3 3 8 - 4 0 6 5

The best way to look powerful in front of your class is to use "Enforceable Statements." Don't tell them what to do, tell them what you will do instead.

*"I listen to one person at a time...
thanks" works much better than,
"Be quiet!"*

Love and Logic Institute, Inc. • 1-800-338-4065

The best way to look weak in front of your class is to tell a strong-willed kid what to do. You'll never win this power struggle.

No statues have ever been built to commemorate critical teachers.

Kids who grow up with criticism become critical adults. Kids who grow up with positives become positive adults.

*Teachers who make a habit of sending kids
to the principal for discipline become teachers
whose students view them as weak.*

Love and Logic Institute, Inc. • 1 - 8 0 0 - 3 3 8 - 4 0 6 5

A very kind and powerful teacher once said to her students: "In my classroom you never have to worry about me sending you to the principal...but there might be days you'll beg me to."

In what way would you like students to get their control needs met in your classroom?
a. Argue, complain, and turn your face red.
b. Refuse to do any work.
c. Make lots of little choices about issues that don't cause a problem for anyone.

Love and Logic Institute, Inc. • 1-800-338-4065

*When a student rejects a teacher's
friendliness, what is he/she really saying?
"I'm really scared to get close.
But…please…don't give up on me!"*

Love and Logic Institute, Inc. • www.loveandlogic.com

There is nothing that defiant students love more than to see angry and frustrated teachers.

Love and Logic Institute, Inc. • 1-800-338-4065

Challenging students are like
copier machines…they can sense
when we're the most stressed…
and choose to self-destruct
at that very moment.

Wise teachers never let their copier
machines...or their students...
see them sweat.

Love and Logic teachers have been known to ask, "Should I put up with that behavior just because I like you? Thanks for stopping."

Love and Logic Institute, Inc. • www.loveandlogic.com

Successful people focus most of their energy on their strengths, so they have the energy to face their weaknesses.

Love and Logic Institute, Inc. • 1-800-338-4065

When a child says, "It's too hard—
I can't do it," the wise teacher smiles
and whispers, "Aren't you glad
I don't believe that?"

Love and Logic Institute, Inc. • 1-800-338-4065

*There is nothing wrong with a difficult student
that a little praise won't make worse.*

Effective teachers replace praise
(e.g., "Wow, that is so great!")
with very specific encouragement
(e.g., "You got eight out of ten
answers correct").

*When a student walks in late,
experiment with whispering in a very
sincere manner, "I'm glad you made it.
We were worried."*

Tardiness is solved through positive relationships NOT punishment.

*Kids work harder for teachers
who smile.*

Love and Logic Institute, Inc. • 1-800-338-4065

*Wise teachers know that checkmarks
on the board are a waste of good chalk.*

Love and Logic teachers strive to give 99%
of their attention to students who are
behaving well. They send the message,
"The way you get attention in this class is
by acting sweet…not sour."

*Schools that provide friendly supervision
have students who are too busy bonding
with adults to vandalize and bully. Schools
that provide stern guards have kids who
become too sneaky to catch.*

Effective teachers ask questions.
Ineffective teachers issue commands.

*Wise teachers know that chores
at home are the cornerstone of
achievement at school.*

Love and Logic Institute, Inc. • www.loveandlogic.com

Children either live up to...or down to...
our expectations.

Love and Logic Institute, Inc. • 1-800-338-4065

Wise teachers know that the vast
majority of our expectations
are communicated by how we act…
not what we say.

*Human beings put more weight on
negative information. Wise teachers
balance every piece of corrective
feedback with ten positives.*

Love and Logic Institute, Inc. • 1-800-338-4065

Effective teachers create predictable routines for their classes. From the first day of school, their students know how to behave while entering class, walking in the hall, etc.

Love and Logic Institute, Inc. • www.loveandlogic.com

Ineffective teachers have no routines...
and lots of stress in their lives.

Love and Logic Institute, Inc. • 1-800-338-4065

Teachers who yell
have smaller voices than
teachers who whisper.

Love and Logic Institute, Inc. • www.loveandlogic.com

When a kid says, "This is boring"
experiment with grinning and saying,
"I know. And if you think it's boring
now, wait until two o'clock!"

*When a student says, "I'm stupid"
experiment with whispering, "Aren't
you glad that I don't believe that?"
and walking away.*

Love and Logic Institute, Inc. • www.loveandlogic.com

*When a student is having a bad day,
experiment with asking, "I forgot to give this
overdue book to the librarian. Will you do me a
favor and run it back for me?"*

*Wise teachers have plenty of
near-overdue books on their desks.*

When a kid whines, "Is this going to be on the test?" smart teachers smile and answer with enthusiasm, "Won't it be exciting to find out!"

Love and Logic Institute, Inc. • www.loveandlogic.com

When a child says, "You're weird"
Love and Logic teachers ask with a
puzzled smile, "It's taken you this
long to figure that out?"

*There's nothing wrong with a student
that a little teacher-student arguing
can't make worse.*

Important research finding!
It is significantly harder for a student
to have a power struggle with a
teacher...when the teacher is not
there. Wise adults walk away from
defiant kids before they get "hooked."

Love and Logic Institute, Inc. • 1 - 8 0 0 - 3 3 8 - 4 0 6 5

Ask your students, "Am I the strictest teacher in this school?" If they answer, "No," say, "I'm so sorry. I must be slipping. I'll get to work on that right away!"

Our wish for you:
That the students in your class will think,
"That's the strictest teacher I've ever
known…and I want to be in his/her class!"

Love and Logic Institute, Inc. • 1-800-338-4065

*Consequences preceded by empathy help
children learn healthy cause and effect.
Consequences preceded by anger and lectures
help children learn to be resentful.*

Love and Logic Institute, Inc. • www.loveandlogic.com

Empathy makes the child's poor decision the "bad guy" and helps the teacher remain the "good guy."

*Every time we make excuses for
misbehavior or rescue children
from their poor decisions,
we cripple them more.*

Love and Logic Institute, Inc. • www.loveandlogic.com

Every time we make excuses for misbehavior or rescue children from their poor decisions, we make our communities harder…and sometimes less safe…places to live.

Love and Logic Institute, Inc. • 1-800-338-4065

*Empathy opens the heart
and mind to learning.*

Love and Logic Institute, Inc. • www.loveandlogic.com

*Teachers who say, "Students don't
have to like me…they just have
to respect me" end each day with
many battle scars.*

Love and Logic Institute, Inc. • 1-800-338-4065

Lecturing a student, "If you'd just behave yourself on the playground, you wouldn't keep getting kicked off" is about as effective as lecturing a spouse, "If you'd just behave yourself in the car, you wouldn't keep getting these tickets."

Love and Logic teachers don't lecture children about their misbehavior. They say few words while letting empathy and consequences do the teaching.

Love and Logic Institute, Inc. • 1 - 8 0 0 - 3 3 8 - 4 0 6 5

*A wise high-school teacher once said
to her class of seniors, "Each Friday,
I grade papers handed in on time. I get
to the late papers during the summer."*

"How are we supposed to graduate if you grade them during the summer?" was answered with a smile and, *"Not to worry. At this school, we offer twelfth grade every year."*

Great teachers are always asking themselves, "If the tables were turned, how would I want to be treated by my teacher?"

If it weren't for wonderful teachers,
we wouldn't have the skills to write
this book…and you wouldn't have
the skills to finish it!

Love and Logic Institute, Inc. • 1-800-338-4065

Also by Jim Fay

Helicopters, Drill Sergeants and Consultants
Four Steps to Responsibility
Love Me Enough to Set Some Limits
I've Got What It Takes
Tickets to Success
Trouble-Free Teens
Pearls of Love and Logic for Parents and Teachers
Putting Parents at Ease

With Charles Fay, Ph.D.

Love and Logic Magic for Early Childhood
Love and Logic Magic: When Kids Leave You Speechless
Teacher in Charge
Calming the Chaos
Hope for Underachieving Kids
Love and Logicisms: Wise Words About Kids

By Charles Fay, Ph.D.

Oh Great! What Do I Do Now?
Angry & Oppositional Students: Calming Classrooms with Love and Logic

Additional copies of this book are available through

Love and Logic Institute, Inc.
2207 Jackson Street
Golden, Colorado 80401-2300

Call or visit our Web site to order our complete catalog
of stress-free parenting and teaching titles.

1-800-338-4065

www.loveandlogic.com

Love and Logic Seminars

Jim Fay and Charles Fay, Ph.D. present
Love and Logic seminars and personal appearances
for both parents and educators in
many cities each year.

For more information,
contact the Love and Logic Institute, Inc. at:

1-800-338-4065

or visit our Web site:

www.loveandlogic.com